D1797404

AND NO SOUND REMEMBERED

Writ

MIGRATION

We rose from the tunnel under the river

As once we did from the sea,

And the mist was hanging over the grey fields,

Waiting, knowing we must come,

As we had done for so many centuries;

And I remember a bleak white Sun

Piercing a round hole in the roof of the sky –

Or was it the pupil of a vast eye, staring?

And suddenly, we were sailing with the tide,

Flowing through the current of liquid air;

There were shoals and schools, and herds of us,

Moving in mute instinctive migration

Towards the first light of the sea,

For in our cells, I feel the terrible cold,

Cold as eyes of glass, so cold,

And the wind is singing in our bones

As the slow procession shuffles

To that shivering place

Where all roads meet.

we rose from the tunnel   under the river

as once we did   from the sea

and the mist was hanging   over the grey fields

waiting knowing   we must come

as we had done   for so many centuries

and I remember

a bleak white sun

piercing a round hole

in the roof of the sky

or was it the pupil

of a vast eye staring

and suddenly we were   sailing with the tide

flowing through the current   of liquid air

there were shoals and schools

and herds of us

moving   in mute instinctive migration

towards the first light   of the sea for

in our cells   I feel

the terrible cold   cold as time fixed at zero

cold as eyes of glass   so cold

and the wind is singing in our bones   as the slow procession shuffles to

that shivering place
where all roads
meet

Co-ordinates

Misty, my breath on the mirror

Reminds me of my mortality;

Spreading, it blots out the animated object

Whose amazing lifelike motions

And depth of 3D being

Can never be truly recorded by artificial instruments;

Panoramic! – The scene behind me becomes alive! –

Alive in the sense of being seen –

Distance! The sheer distance and dizzy complication of it all

Assaults my understanding brain

And the pigeons fly from their blown compartments;

Into the metaphorical air

As I verbally retch into the dull basin beneath;

For how could I, in my hopeless and hindsight days

Ever hope to see

That the child I scolded so severely

Was already a dying and divided thing,

Long past the fixed but withering co-ordinate

Of my censuring hand?

MISTY – My breath on/ the MIRROR

Reminds me/off my MORTALITY

S P R E A D I N G -

IT BLOTS OUT the animated object

Whose amazing LIELIE MTINS
f k oo

And DEPTH of

3
D being

Recorded

Can never be truly

by ARTIFICIAL INSTRUMENTS

PANORAMIC! the scene behind ME !

becomes alive ALIVE !

at least in the sense of being SEEN

D I S T A N C E !

The sheer d i s t a n c e

z
I Z

and   D   Y c!o*mpLi6#t-ion of it all

Assaults my understanding brain

Y
l
f

And the pigeons

blown

From their   compartments
Into the metaphorical air
As I verbally retch
IntoThe dull basin beneath

For how could I
In my hopeless and hindsight days
Ever hope to see
That the child I scolded so severely
Was already a dying and divided thing
Lost past the fixed but withering co-ordinate
Of my censoring hand?

SPECTATOR

I wander through the vast theatre

A mere spectator,

Where forgotten actors curtain calls

Ring from the back doors through deserted stalls.

Along a long corridor

A sound like glass bells tumbling in a sleepy head,

Wakes the crystal ghosts

Whose voices from a dark and windy Winter hall

Bring to life all the shadows formed on a black and white night

With a soundtrack that whispers like a silhouette.

The empty chairs and I laugh and cry

Through a comical scene

Where a running boy trips over a bicycle

Catching his feet between the broken wheels

Chained forever to the past.

Then, the uneasy moments, for that boy is gone now,

And will never be seen again.......

Will never.....never....can anyone understand never?

Now, no-one in the street, and from my seat

The film flickers and fails in sudden falling blackness....and silence..

And though it returns and flows in smooth reassurance

My mind begins to wander away

For I know how it must predictably end...

So as the warm lights shower the town

And the houses drown in the long streets

All through the raining night,

I leave to find that dark road leading home.

I WANDER THROUGH THE VAST THEATRE
A MERE SPECTATOR
WHERE FORGOTTEN ACTORS CURTAIN
CALLS
RING FROM THE BACK DOORS
THROUGH DESERTED STALLS

ALONG	A	LONG	CORRIDOR
A	SOUND		
	LIKE		
	GLASS		
	BELLS	TUMBLING	IN A
			SLEEPY HEAD
			WAKES
			THE
		CRYSTAL	GHOSTS
			WHOSE
		VOICES	
		FROM	
		A	
		DARK	
		AND	
		WINDY	
WINTER HALL	BRING		
	TO		
	LIFE		
	ALL		
	THE		SHADOWS
			FORMED
			ON
			A
			BLACK
			AND
			WHITE
		NIGHT	
WITH		A SOUNDTRACK	
		THAT WHISPERS	
		LIKE	
		A	SILHOUETTE

THE LIGHT SPRINGS LIKE A FOUNTAIN
AS

THE			
EMPTY	CHAIRS	AND	I
	LAUGH	AND	CRY
	THROUGH		
	A		
COMICAL	SCENE		
	WHERE		
	A		
RUNNING	BOY		
	FALLS OVER		
	A		
	BICYCLE		
	CATCHING		
	HIS		
	FEET		BETWEEN
			THE
			BROKEN
			WHEELS
CHAINED	FOREVER		
TO			
THE			
PAST			

Then.........the uneasy moments
For that boy is gone now
And will never be seen again.....

Will never......
        Never..........
Can anyone understand never?

Now
No-one   in the streets
    And   from my seat   the film flickers and fails
                                In   sudden   falling

BLACKNESS
BLACKNESS

And................................silence.

And though
It returns   and   flows
        In
Smooth reassurance

wander

My mind begins to   away.................

For I know how it must predictably end.

So as the warm lights   shower   the town

drown

And the houses   in the long streets

All through the raining night
I leave
To find that dark road
Leading home.

AND NO SOUND REMEMBERED

And when I arrived, the door was locked and no-one there,

And in the empty parks, the swings had been taken down,

And no sound remembered

All the children whose quiet voices are scattered

In every corner of the earth,

Washed away in the rain,

As if I was never born on that clear morning

When no-one in the World knew me;

As if I had never grown in the schools and hills of a Village

That seemed to dream in the Sunlight of the High field.

Where standing now I see the light from the same Sun

Reach low across the roofs of streets where we ran

With no sense of the Sun's journey;

And never to look in a window on that same street, now solid,

With Summer closing, and the shadows long;

And never to see this face;

And never to see these images of my Mother and Father,

Telling bedtime stories, teaching prayers, and saying goodnight..

And no sound remembered

All the children, scattered and voiceless,

Gone forever, and never to be seen or heard

In the pale light of this dying afternoon.

AND WHEN I ARRIVED   THE DOOR   was   LOCKED   and   NO-ONE THERE

AND   in   THE   EMPTY

                                        PARKS

                                        THE SWINGS   had been   TAKEN DOWN   and   NO SOUND
REMEMBERED ALL   THE CHILDREN

WHOSE QUIET VOICES ARE   SCATTERED

IN EVERY CORNER   of   THE EARTH   WASHED AWAY

                          in   THE RAIN

AS IF I   was   NEVER BORN

                          on   THAT CLEAR MORNING   when   NO-ONE

                          In   THE WORLD

KNEW   me

AS IF I HAD   NEVER GROWN

                          in   THE SCHOOLS

                          and   HILLS

                          of   A VILLAGE   that

SEEMED TO DREAM   in   THE SUNLIGHT

                          of   THE HIGH FIELD

  Where

STANDING NOW I SEE   THE LIGHT

                    from   THE SAME SUN   reach
                                                   low

                    across   THE ROOFS
                    of   STREETS

WHERE WE RAN   with   NO SENSE

                    of   THE SUNS JOURNEY   and   NEVER TO LOOK
                    in   A WINDOW
                    on   THAT SAME STREET   now   SOLID
                    with   SUMMER   CLOSING
                    and   THE SHADOWS   long

                                                   and   NEVER TO SEE

                             THIS FACE   and   NEVER TO SEE

                             THESE IMAGES
                    of   MY MOTHER
                    and   FATHER
                    telling BEDTIME STORIES
                    teaching PRAYERS
        and   saying   GOODNIGHT   and   NO SOUND

REMEMBERED   all   THE CHILDREN   SCATTERED

                                                   and   VOICELESS
                                                           GONE FOREVER
                                                   and   NEVER TO BE SEEN
                                                           OR HEARD

                    in   THE PALE LIGHT

                    of   THIS DYING AFTERNOON

Mother

When I was cold   in the night

You came to me and   your warm hand

Brushed the darkness

Back to the corners

Of the room

You laughed and   chased away the fevers

                                         Of a young mind and

I slept like you said and   when I woke

In the morning   the Sun was there

                                         Just as you had promised

I leapt out into the long day

To the trees and fields

And playgrounds of the people

Who rattle like toys   in the locked Summers

                                         Of my childhood

And though the Sun disappeared

Again that night

My faith in you

Kept the darkness away

Mother

I am that child   again

And I would gladly run   through the strange years

To hide in your warmth but   My faith has gone and

The darkness

17

Creeps from the corners

Of this cold room

Where I was always alone

EDWARD

My Son,

Your life's remains

Lie trapped beneath the soil;

It would ease my mind to believe

That somewhere, beyond this life,

Where joy is a fable,

You had found peace;

But my eyes do not see you,

And the World is so empty.

Where are the days we were to share,

Where is the life you are denied,

It would ease my mind to believe

That somewhere, beyond this life,

Where tears are mandatory,

We will meet again;

But I saw your face

Before the darkness

Closed on you forever.

MY CLOCKWORK SOLDIER

My clockwork soldier lies far from the playroom,

Rusted beyond belief;

In his metal death, he lies,

Locked forever

At the moment of final capitulation.

He sees nothing, did he ever see?

Nothing? Nothing? Feel?

Was he a figment of a child's mind?

A ghost from a room so long forgotten,

Lost in the archives of chalk-riddled blackboard years?

Or somewhere, in the bodiless corridors of nowhere,

Does he wander crying endless tears.

And this is not like sleep,

Not like that drifting, insensible

Unconscious travelling through time;

No longer guarded,

The whirring heart which has beat its pendulum

Through the long spinning minutes of hours and days and weeks,

Feathers to a halt,

And silence rules the inner man.

Now we must move on and leave him,

For he is caught in the utterance – caught

In the absolute cessation of his mortal self,

And we must move on –

We must.

For when that warm halo, life,

Cools and disappears,

Leaving only bacteria

The World's true and most natural heirs,

When the Sun's long journey ends

And darkens your Roman numeral skies,

Then the hands say it's time, my soldier,

To close your clockwork eyes.

MY CLOCKWORK   SOLDIER

LIES   FAR FROM   THE PLAYROOM

RUSTED   BEYOND   BELIEF

IN HIS METAL   DEATH   HE LIES   LOCKED FOREVER

AT THE MOMENT

OF

FINAL CAPITULATION

AND THIS IS NOT LIKE SLEEP

NOT LIKE THAT

DRIFTING

INSENSIBLE UNCONSCIOUS

TRAVELLING

THROUGH

TIME   NO LONGER GUARDED

THE

WHIRRING HEART   WHICH HAS BEAT

ITS

PENDULUM

THROUGH THE LONG SPINNING

MINUTES

OF

HOURS

AND

DAYS

AND

WEEKS

FEATHERS TO A HALT   AND   SILENCE RULES

THE INNER MAN   NOW WE MUST MOVE ON

AND

LEAVE HIM

FOR HE IS CAUGHT

IN THE UTTERANCE

CAUGHT

IN THE ABSOLUTE CESSATION

OF HIS MORTAL SELF

AND WE

MUST MOVE ON

WE MUST

For
when
that
warm   halo   life
                                                 cools
                                                          and   disappears
                          leaving
                          only

bacteria   the
                          Worlds
                          true
                          and
                          most
                          natural
                          heirs   when
the   Sun's
             long
             journey
             ends   and
                                         Darkens   your
                                                              Roman
                                                              Numeral
                                                              skies
                                                              then
                                                              the
                                                              hands
                                                              Say   its
                         Time
                         My soldier   to
                                                             close
                                                             your   clockwork
                                                             eyes

STILL ROOMS

Still rooms and empty chairs are everywhere,

The silence of people who played in the park

Till the cemetery bells rang at dark,

Sleepy green and moist with rain,

Children come home,

Come home again.

The restless Sun disturbed the seeds,

The warm earth sheltered among the weeds,

From each Spring bulb of each Winter bone,

Growing together, but always alone,

For deep in their shadows,

All through the long day,

Time with his walking stick,

Whittling away.

This is dark country, my home,

The sky unwinds in the song I've known

Since the meadows stretched through long Summer days,

And time left me here, in this strange place,

Ringing in my ears, the rhythm of the tune,

This confusion of breathing in a sleeping room.

Somewhere lost in blackest night,

In that meadow, now closed to light,

A name is carved on the neutral stone,

And though that name is the name I've known

These many years, I let it pass,

And sing my songs through the sound of grass.

And I will sing till the bells at dark eclipse

The Sun forever, and daylight slips

Away, for children and parks must cease

To be, and circles ever decrease,

Till wandering through these arcades of mine,

The slot-machine Sun runs out of time.

STILL | ROOMS and | EMPTY CHAIRS

SILENT | CITIES | | | EVERYWHERE

The SILENCE of | PEOPLE

| who PLAYED | In the PARK

| TILL

The CEMETERY | BELLS RANG | | | At DARK

| SLEEPY GREEN | | And

| | MOIST WITH RAIN | | CHILDREN
COME HOME

COME HOME

AGAIN

THE RESTLESS
SUN DISTURBED

The SEEDS   THE WARM EARTH

SHELTERED   AMONG the WEEDS

From EACH   SPRING

BULB

Of EACH   WINTER

BONE   GROWING

TOGETHER but

ALWAYS ALONE

for   DEEP in

Their SHADOWS

ALL THROUGH the   TIME   With his WALKING   WHITTLING AWAY
LONG DAY   STICK

28

This is DARK

COUNTRY

                                                                                    MY HOME

                                            The SKY UNWINDS
                                            in the SONG I've
                                            known since the
                                            MEADOWS

STRETCHED
through LONG
SUMMER DAYS and

                                                                TIME LEFT ME   HERE in this
RINGING   STRANGE PLACE

In my EARS

                            The RHYTHM of the

                            TUNE

This CONFUSION

                            Of BREATHING

                                                                In a SLEEPING
                                                                ROOM

somewhere LOST in   BLACKEST NIGHT

In that MEADOW   NOW CLOSED to

LIGHT

A NAME IS CARVED   On the NEUTRAL

STONE

And though that
NAME is the NAME
I'VE KNOWN these
many years I

LET IT PASS

And

SING my SONGS
through

The SOUND of
GRASS

And

I WILL SING TILL

The BELLS at DARK
ECLIPSE the SUN

FOREVER

And the DAYLIGHT

SLIPS AWAY

For CHILDREN and
PARKS must CEASE
to be

And CIRCLES ever

DECREASE

Till wandering
through these
ARCADES of mine

The SLOT-MACHINE

SUN

Runs out of TIME

GURGLE GURGLE

Before we go gurgle gurgle to the grave,

Let me take you down below the coral reef,

Where on this Island of time

We float in our silent way.

Don't worry,

The air in this suit is good for seventy odd years,

Barring accidents and acts of God.

These people we pass soundless in the streets

Are only poor sailors like yourself,

Only poor assorted sailors

Submerged in this strange Atlantis of a City.

Every evening, as the rays of the red Sun

Run over the water, we sit here on the verandah,

Breathing the cool blue-green,

Watching the insects dip and swim

Between the waves of light and night,

Catching the day in fishermen's nets

As she sinks to her sombre rest.

While the tide takes us away to play in the sand –

Oh happy donkey-riding flag-waving sandcastle Summers!

And the time ever turning, changing, unending,

The wind growing colder,

Sending shivering droves to San Mauritz,

Growing older, the Sun burning out,

Spending Autumn and Winter in brown dead-leaf houses,

Withering, winding down, the Sun pale in the sky,

And why anyway?

Don't worry, not now, but one day

I will take my raft to the edge of the sea

And drift away......

Till then, breathe deep, and let me take you down

Below the coral reef

Where on this Island of time

We float in our silent way;

At least till He who keeps the oxygen flowing

While we dive in the deep waters of the World

Calls and end to all our play.

Before we go   <u>Gurgle Gurgle</u>   *to*   *the*   Grave
Let me
Take you   Down below   The Coral   Reef

where
On   This   Island   *Of*   Time   We Float
in our   Silent   Way
Don't worry   *the*   Air   *In*   This   Suit   Is good
for   Seventy   Odd   Years

Barring
Accidents   *and*   Acts   *Of*   God
these   People   We pass   Soundless   In the
      Street
Are only   Poor   Sailors   Like
      Yourself

only   Poor   Assorted
      Sailors

Submerged   *In*   This   Strange   Atlantis
      Of
      A City

EveryEvening   *As*   *the*   Rays
      Of
      The Red Sun
      Run   Over
      The
      Water

We sit here
On the
Verandah   Breathing   *the*   Cool   Blue-green
Watching   *The*   Insects   Dip&swim

Between
The waves
Of
Light & Night   Catching   The Day   *In*   Fishermen's
      Nets

as
She   Sinks
      To
      Her
      Sombre Rest

while

The Tide   *takes*

     Us   Away to Play   In the Sand

            Oh Happy   Donkey-Riding

                                 Flag-Waving   Sandcastle

                                                  Summers!

And

The Time

     ever   Turning

            Changing

            Unending

The Wind   Growing   Colder

            Sending   Shivering

                                 Droves   To

                                          San Mauritz

            Growing   Older

The Sun

            Burning   Out

            Spending   Autumn

                                   And

                                   Winter

                          In   Brown

                                   Dead-leaf

                                   Houses

            Withering   Winding Down

                             In

                           The Sky

                           And

                           Why

                           Anyway?

Don't Worry Not Now I will take My Raft

But One Day

To

the Edge

Of

The Sea

.....Away And drift...

Till then

Breathe Deep

And Let me

take you

Down Below The Coral Reef

where

On This Island Of

Time We Float

In our Silent Way

At least till

HE

Who keeps

The

Oxygen

Flowing while We Dive

In the

Deep Waters

Of the World

Calls an End

To All our Play

STANDING IN THE RAIN

Dark days fill the sky

Birds are flying over fields that cry.

When Winter ends,

The weak Sun stretches in the pale trees,

And Summer comes.

And as the seasons grind along

The characters on the wheel

The calendars turn through years printed with people,

Churning us out

In Towns and Cities that shout

And sprawl and die

As blackened daylight ends

The flat discoloured rain-battered boxes

Of matchstick men;

Shapes with sounds

Whose smudged inkspot faces

Collide with my unreal eyes

In shadowy sidestreets that pass with no comment.

The World is so still beneath the noise

Is anyone there?

But there is no shelter in these half-formed houses that fade

In the melting light,

And the lamp-posts march to the night

In time's own time

Through streets that never knew

Names they drowned as cars drive slowly

All the way down the avenue.

Are we the charcoal figures seen on the kerb?

Are we the bus-stop ghosts

Soaked through to the skin and bone,

Scarecrows standing in the rain

And utterly alone.

If you are above me and love me,

Then free me, dissolve me in this sea

Where I never dying drown.

STANDING IN THE RAIN

THE WEAK SUN
STRETCHES IN THE

1.

DARK	DAYS FILL THE	SKY
FIELDS		BIRDS
PALE	TREES	THAT CRY
		ARE FLYING OVER
		WHEN WINTER ENDS
		AND SUMMER COMES.

2.

AND AS THE SEASONS GRIND ALONG THE WORLD IS SO STILL BENEATH THE NOISE
THE CHARACTERS ON THE WHEEL - IS ANYONE THERE?
THE CALENDARS TURN THROUGH YEARS PRINTED WITH PEOPLE BUT THERE IS NO SHELTER IN THESE HALF-FORMED HOUSES THAT FADE

4.

CHURNING US OUT IN THE MELTING LIGHT
IN TOWNS AND CITIES THAT SHOUT AND THE LAMP-POSTS MARCH TO THE NIGHT
AND SPRAWL AND DIE IN TIME'S OWN TIME
AS BLACKENED DAYLIGHT ENDS THROUGH STREETS THAT NEVER KNEW
THE FLAT DISCOLOURED RAIN-BATTERED BOXES NAMES THEY DROWNED AS CARS DRIVE SLOWLY
CONTAINING MATCHSTICK MEN ALL THE WAY DOWN THE AVENUE

3.

SHAPES
SMUDGED

UNREAL
SHADOWY

WITH
INKSPOT

EYES

SOUNDS WHOSE
FACES COLLIDE

WITH MY

IN
SIDESTREETS
THAT PASS
WITH NO COMMENT

5.

ARE WE THE

BUS STOP

GHOSTS

CHARCOAL

FIGURES

SOAKED THROUGH

SEEN ON THE KERB

ARE WE THE

SKIN AND BONE

TO THE

SCARECROWS

STANDING
IN THE RAIN
AND

UTTERLY ALONE

6.

IF YOU ARE ABOVE ME AND LOVE ME
THEN FREE ME, DISSOLVE ME IN THIS SEA
WHERE I NEVER DYING DROWN

CLOSING

Lord, this evening is closing,

And screwed down inside my wooden mind,

I can feel tomorrow rising like a shroud

Over the unbelievable hills.

(You see – it's useless,

It's all lost in this stupid drunken night,

And the words run out of letters and syllables –

But this is as it should be,

For the best words are the ones you never write,

And the spluttering ink spoils)

The pure pain

That cries like a confused child

In the crude earth of the smothering womb.

Oh Dear Lord!

Let this throat of an evening

Choke on the red World

And close a chapter of worthless words.

LORD
THIS
EVENING
IS

AND

TOMORROW
RISING
LIKE
THE
UNBELIEVABLE
HILLS

OVER

I CAN FEEL

MY
MIND

CLOSING
INSIDE
A

SCREWED DOWN
WOODEN
SHROUD

(YOU SEE—IT'S USELESS, IT'S ALL LOST IN THIS STUPID DRUNKEN NIGHT

AND THE WORDS RUN OUT OF LETTERS AND SYLLABLES –BUT THIS IS AS IT
SHOULD BE, FOR THE BEST WORDS ARE THE ONES YOU NEVER WRITE, AND THE

THE PURE PAIN

THAT CRIES
LIKE
A
CONFUSED
CHILD

OF AN EVENING

OH
DEAR LORD!
LET THIS
THROAT

OF THE
SMOTHERING
WOMB

CLOSE
A CHAPTER

ON
THE RED WORLD

AND

OF
WORTHLESS
WORDS

CHOKE

IN THE
CRUDE
EARTH

BEGINNING

What part of me sailed with my Father's sperm?

Across the wild sea to the grave of my Mother's egg?

Shining like a pearl, the World she gave to the children,

Naked and unborn,

Who wait for life to begin.

And stirred by the chiming of a synchronised hour,

Did I wake in the steepled church to climb on a seed of light,

Spinning like a star through the heart of time

Where the blood combines

To begin the long journey to morning.

And together, we grow, the earth breathing,

The red rivers running in the limbs of the high trees,

Moving, flowing like the Sun through the attic sky,

And the darkness flies from the morning of my days,

For I am alive!

Sitting quiet in a solid room,

The streets are still now,

And the gathering clouds have faces,

Drifting like the Moon

Through my Mother and Father and me,

Endlessly drifting,

Never to be born to this World.

And chosen by the storm of that fierce month,

I pierced the burning rain

And the red neck of the womb,

Closing like a clam on the child's head....

In innocence, I entered the World,

Knowing nothing of limits or......time....

Never seeing in the blindness of my Father's hand

That the Sun was weak and dark

In the cave of the fertile earth,

Growing like the grass on a closed grave,

Or that wrapped in the colours of time,

I was falling to an ocean of silence.....

What part of me **Sailed** with my Father's **Sperm**

Across the wild **Sea** to the **grave** of my Mother's **egg**

Shining like a **Pearl**   The world she gave to the children

Naked and unborn

Who wait for **Life !**   to begin

And stirred by the chiming of a synchronised *hour* **hour**

Did I wake in the steepled **Church** To   climb on

A STEEPLE OF LIGHT

Spinning like a star
Through the heart of time

Where the   combines

To begin the long journey to   morning

And together we grow, the  breathing

The red rivers running, flowing like  Through the attic sky

And the darkness flies from the morning Of my days, for I am

Sitting quiet in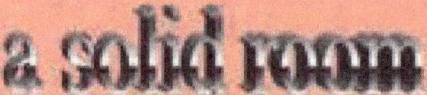

The streets are still now
And the gathering clouds have faces

Through my Mother and Father and me,
Endlessly drifting
Never to be born to this world.

And chosen by the  of that fierce month

I pierced
And the red neck of the womb

Closing like a Clam

on the child's head
In innocence, I entered the world

Knowing nothing of limits or

Never seeing in the blindness of my Father's hand

That the sun was weak and dark in the cave of the **fertile**   earth

Growing like the   *grass*   On a closed grave

Or that wrapped in the   **colours**   of time

I was falling to   **an ocean of silence**

NOTES TO THE POEMS

Words have no significance or very little life in themselves; they exist to convey, as best they can, the abstract emotions we feel inside our hearts and minds. No words can ever accurately or totally illustrate those feelings, abstract and multi-dimensional things that do not consist of words, but of unformed, merging, and conflicting messages pulsing through our brains and into our souls. More often than not, it takes many combinations of words to attempt to find the true meaning of what we are feeling, and to do it well enough to give whoever is reading or listening the best chance of feeling something of what we feel.

To that purpose, these poems attempt to add a further dimension to a flat page of words, in the hope that they help to build a more thorough portrait of what is behind the words themselves. The poems can be read in several ways; the main body of each poem is meant to be read in conventional style, left to right, line following line; but most of the poems can also be read in alternative ways, quite often each section being read top to bottom, as if in columns. Each alternative reading or part is intended to give another meaning to the poem, without deviating from the central intention of the piece. For instance, in "Migration", each 'wing' should be read top to bottom without reference to the other 'wing' until the meeting of the words in the centre and at the end. In "Still Rooms", each verse can also be read in columns, top to bottom, but every verse is interchangeable and can be read in any sequence, 4,2,5,1,3; 5,2,3,1,4; etc, and the columns themselves are also interchangeable, giving alternative impulses to the expression intended in the main body of the poem. As well as being read left to right, the second verse of "My Clockwork Soldier" should be read top to bottom in columns, each column to be read in sequence, making a completely alternative reading, but with the same intrinsic meaning.

Each poem has its own structure, and sometimes consists of images intended to enhance or illustrate the emotion underlying the words. The poems, of course, can be read conventionally, and each poem is set out for that purpose prior to the Rubik version that follows.

Writ; Hertfordshire 2019

CPSIA information can be obtained
at www.ICGtesting.com
Printed in the USA
BVHW010948040219
539410BV00002B/2/P

9 781838 530853